Chock Full of
•CHOCOLATE•

Written by Elizabeth MacLeod

Illustrated by June Bradford

KIDS CAN PRESS

With love to Alix, John, Malcolm and Victoria
— true chocolate lovers

Text © 2005 Elizabeth MacLeod
Illustrations © 2005 June Bradford

KIDS CAN DO IT and the 🎨 logo are trademarks of Kids Can Press Ltd.

Kids Can Press acknowledges the financial support of the Government of Ontario, through the Ontario Media Development Corporation's Ontario Book Initiative, and the Government of Canada, through the BPIDP, for our publishing activity.

Published in Canada by
Kids Can Press Ltd.
29 Birch Avenue
Toronto, ON M4V 1E2

Published in the U.S. by
Kids Can Press Ltd.
2250 Military Road
Tonawanda, NY 14150

www.kidscanpress.com

Edited by Lori Burwash
Designed by Kathleen Collett and Karen Powers

Printed and bound in China

The hardcover edition of this book is smyth sewn casebound.
The paperback edition of this book is limp sewn with a drawn-on cover.

CM 05 0 9 8 7 6 5 4 3 2 1
CM PA 05 0 9 8 7 6 5 4 3 2 1

Library and Archives Canada Cataloguing in Publication

MacLeod, Elizabeth
Chock full of chocolate / written by Elizabeth MacLeod ; illustrated by June Bradford.

(Kids can do it)
Includes index.
ISBN 1-55337-762-1 (bound).   ISBN 1-55337-763-X (pbk.)

1. Cookery (Chocolate) — Juvenile literature. 2. Chocolate — Juvenile literature.
I. Bradford, June II. Title. III. Series.

TX767.C5M32 2005   j641.6'374   C2004-906037-6

Kids Can Press is a *Corus*™ Entertainment company

Contents

Introduction

From ancient Mexico to outer space, chocolate's been there! The Aztec people were slurping hot chocolate more than 700 years ago. Today, chocolate's included on space flights because it gives astronauts a quick energy boost — and tastes so good, too.

This book includes recipes for classic chocolate treats, cookies and squares, desserts especially for parties, and gifts for chocolate lovers. You'll also find decorating ideas to make your chocolate treats look extra special. All the recipes are fun, easy — and chock full of chocolate!

MEASURING INGREDIENTS

Both the metric and imperial systems of measurement are used in this book. The systems are different, so choose one and use it for all your measuring.

Wet ingredients and dry ingredients require different measuring cups. A wet measuring cup has a spout to make pouring easier.

A dry measuring cup is flat across the top so you can use a knife to level off the ingredients for an accurate measure.

If you're making a treat for someone, make sure he or she isn't allergic to any of the ingredients, such as nuts or dairy products. Always carefully clean your utensils and work surface after making each recipe.

CUTTING OUT COOKIE DOUGH

Put a large piece of wax paper on a table or countertop. (A dab of water under each corner will hold the paper in place.) Sprinkle a little flour on the wax paper and on a rolling pin.

Place dough on the wax paper and roll it out to the thickness suggested in the recipe. Cut out the cookies with a cookie cutter dipped in flour. Use a lifter to transfer cookies to a prepared baking sheet. Combine leftover dough, roll again and repeat until you've used all the dough.

BAKING COOKIES AND SQUARES

You'll find it faster and easier to make cookies if you use several baking sheets. It's also a good idea to use baking sheets and pans lined with aluminum foil.

Bake cookies, one sheet at a time, in the center of your oven. Most cookies are baked when slightly firm to the touch. Squares are done when they're slightly firm in the middle and have pulled away from the sides of the pan.

BAKING MUFFINS, CAKES AND LOAVES

Bake muffins, cakes and loaves in the center of your oven. Muffins are baked when the middle springs back when gently touched. A cake or loaf is done when a toothpick or cake tester inserted into the middle comes out clean and dry — or when the middle springs back when gently touched and the sides have shrunk away from the pan.

BAKING TIMES

Cooking times vary from oven to oven. Bake your treats for the minimum time suggested, then test to see if they're done. If they're not, check again in 1 or 2 minutes. You may want to set a timer to remind you.

MELTING CHOCOLATE AND BUTTER

Chocolate burns easily, so ask an adult to help you melt it in a microwave or double boiler. Heat chocolate slowly, just enough to melt it, stirring frequently.

If using a microwave, use high power and stir the chocolate at least every 30 seconds. If using a double boiler, place it on low heat. You can melt chips, squares or bars — cut up bars to help them melt faster.

Butter should be melted the same way as chocolate. Heat it slowly and get an adult to help you.

Use thick oven mitts to handle hot saucepans or baking sheets and pans. Ask an adult to help move things into and out of the oven.

Chocolate chippers

For chewy cookies, bake these a little less. For crispy cookies, bake slightly longer.

YOU WILL NEED

250 mL	butter (room temperature)	1 c.
175 mL	white sugar	¾ c.
175 mL	brown sugar (lightly packed)	¾ c.
2	eggs	2
10 mL	vanilla	2 tsp.
550 mL	all-purpose flour	2¼ c.
5 mL	baking soda	1 tsp.
2 mL	salt	½ tsp.
375 mL	chocolate chips	1½ c.

large mixing bowl, wooden spoon, small spoon, baking sheet lined with aluminum foil, lifter, cooling rack

1 Preheat the oven to 180°C (350°F).

2 Beat together the butter and sugars until creamy. Stir in the eggs and vanilla. Add the flour, baking soda and salt. Blend well. Stir in the chocolate chips.

3 Drop the dough by spoonfuls onto the baking sheet about 4 cm (1½ in.) apart.

4 Bake 8 to 10 minutes, until golden. Cool 3 minutes, then transfer cookies to the cooling rack. Cool completely.

Store in an airtight container at room temperature for up to 1 week or freeze for up to 2 months.

Makes about 5 dozen cookies

OTHER IDEAS

★ Make bars by spreading the dough in a 23 cm x 33 cm (9 in. x 13 in.) cake pan lined with aluminum foil. Bake at 190°C (375°F) for 25 to 30 minutes, until golden brown. Cool in the pan on the cooling rack.

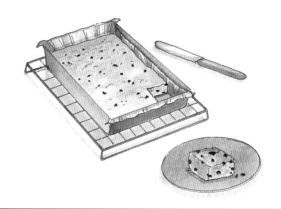

Big-bite brownies

Classic treats with extra chocolate in them.

YOU WILL NEED

4	squares unsweetened chocolate, melted (page 5)	4
175 mL	butter, melted (page 5)	¾ c.
3	eggs	3
375 mL	white sugar	1½ c.
5 mL	vanilla	1 tsp.
175 mL	all-purpose flour	¾ c.
1 mL	salt	¼ tsp.
300 mL	chocolate chips	1¼ c.

small mixing bowl, wooden spoon, large mixing bowl, 20 cm (8 in.) square cake pan lined with aluminum foil, cooling rack

1 Preheat the oven to 180°C (350°F).

2 In the small bowl, mix the chocolate and butter. Refrigerate 15 minutes, until at room temperature.

3 In the large bowl, stir the eggs and sugar until pale yellow. Add the vanilla. Mix in the chocolate mixture until well combined. Gently stir in the flour and salt. Add the chocolate chips. Stir well and pour into the pan.

4 Bake 40 to 45 minutes, until done (page 5). Cool completely in the pan on the cooling rack, then cut into large squares.

Store in an airtight container at room temperature for up to 1 week or freeze for up to 2 months.

Makes about 9 large brownies

DECORATE IT

★ Make patterns on squares or cakes by sifting icing sugar or cocoa powder over doilies or shapes you've made.

Fudgy cake

Before icing the cake, insert clean, foil-wrapped coins in it. Tell your friends to look for surprises!

YOU WILL NEED

375 mL	white sugar	1½ c.
175 mL	butter (room temperature)	¾ c.
3	eggs	3
10 mL	vanilla	2 tsp.
500 mL	all-purpose flour	2 c.
150 mL	unsweetened cocoa powder	⅔ c.
7 mL	baking soda	1½ tsp.
2 mL	baking powder	½ tsp.
325 mL	milk	1⅓ c.

large mixing bowl, wooden spoon, sifter, medium mixing bowl, two 20 cm (8 in.) round cake pans lined with aluminum foil, two cooling racks

1 Preheat the oven to 180°C (350°F).

2 In the large bowl, cream together the sugar and butter until smooth and light in color. Add the eggs and vanilla and beat for 5 minutes.

3 Sift together the flour, cocoa, baking soda and baking powder into the medium bowl.

4 Add one-third of the flour mixture to the butter mixture and mix well. Stir in half the milk.

5 Repeat step 4, then add the remaining flour mixture and mix well. Pour half the batter into each pan. Tap lightly to remove large air bubbles.

6 Bake 35 to 40 minutes, until done (page 5). Cool 15 minutes in the pans on the cooling racks. Then turn the cakes upside down onto the racks and remove from pans and foil. Cool completely.

Store in airtight containers at room temperature for up to 4 days or freeze for up to 1 month.

Makes 8 to 12 servings

Creamy icing

Chocolate icing is perfect for any kind of cake.

YOU WILL NEED		
750 mL	icing sugar	3 c.
250 mL	unsweetened cocoa powder	1 c.
125 mL	butter, melted (page 5)	½ c.
75 mL	milk	⅓ c.
10 mL	vanilla	2 tsp.
	sifter, large mixing bowl, hand or electric mixer	

1 Sift the icing sugar and cocoa into the bowl. Add the butter and use the mixer to cream the ingredients together.

2 Add the milk and vanilla. Beat until smooth.

3 If the icing is too thin, add more icing sugar. If it is too thick, add a little more milk.

Refrigerate in an airtight container for up to 1 week. Mix well before using and add a little milk if necessary.

Makes enough icing to frost a 20 cm (8 in.) layer cake

OTHER IDEAS

★ Add orange or mint flavoring to the icing. Start by adding 4 drops and keep adding until you create the flavor you want.

DECORATE IT

★ Make chocolate triangles to decorate the sides of a cake. Melt 4 squares of semisweet or milk chocolate (page 5) and spread smoothly in a rectangle about 12.5 cm x 33 cm (5 in. x 13 in.) on a baking sheet lined with wax paper. Refrigerate about 15 minutes, until set, then let stand for 5 minutes at room temperature.

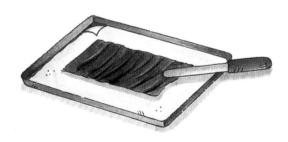

Using a table knife, cut out thin triangles as tall as the cake and place around the iced cake. If you like, use different types of chocolate, such as white and dark, to make different colors of triangles.

Cool shake

The perfect way to chill out on a hot summer day.

YOU WILL NEED

500 mL	cold milk	2 c.
25 mL	unsweetened cocoa powder	2 tbsp.
22 mL	white sugar	1½ tbsp.
500 mL	chocolate ice cream	2 c.
	blender	

1 Place the milk, cocoa and sugar in the blender and blend at medium-high speed for 1 minute.

2 Add the ice cream and whip at medium speed for 30 seconds. Serve immediately.

Makes 2 servings

OTHER IDEAS

★ Add a sliced banana or 125 mL (½ c.) chopped strawberries when you add the ice cream.

★ Add a few drops of orange or peppermint flavoring when you add the ice cream.

★ Use other flavors of chocolate ice cream, such as chocolate mint or chocolate orange.

★ Spoon a dollop of whipped cream onto the milk shake and add chocolate sprinkles. If you like, place a cherry, strawberry or raspberry on top.

Deep dark fudge

A rich, creamy treat with only three ingredients. What could be easier?

YOU WILL NEED

1	300 mL (10 oz.) can sweetened condensed milk	1
750 mL	chocolate chips	3 c.
10 mL	vanilla	2 tsp.

large microwavable bowl, wooden spoon, 20 cm (8 in.) square cake pan lined with aluminum foil

1 Combine the condensed milk and chocolate chips. Microwave on high 3 to 5 minutes, stirring every 90 seconds, until the chocolate is melted. (You can also melt in a double boiler over medium-low heat — be sure to get an adult's help.)

2 Mix in the vanilla. Pour into the pan.

3 Refrigerate 2 hours, until firm.

Refrigerate in an airtight container for up to 2 weeks.

Makes about 2 dozen squares

OTHER IDEAS

★ After you add the vanilla, stir in 125 mL (½ c.) pecans, almonds, butterscotch chips or peanut butter chips.

★ Cut the fudge into squares and place a nut on each one.

★ When the fudge is cool, cut into squares and drizzle melted white chocolate (page 5) on top.

Peppermint bars

Leave out the peppermint and coloring to make tasty treats known as Nanaimo Bars.

YOU WILL NEED

125 mL	butter	½ c.
50 mL	white sugar	¼ c.
1	egg (beaten)	1
75 mL	unsweetened cocoa powder	⅓ c.
500 mL	graham cracker crumbs	2 c.
250 mL	desiccated coconut	1 c.
125 mL	chopped walnuts	½ c.
50 mL	butter (room temperature)	¼ c.
500 mL	icing sugar	2 c.
20 mL	milk	4 tsp.
	peppermint flavoring	
	pink food coloring	
4	squares semisweet chocolate	4
15 mL	butter	1 tbsp.

medium saucepan, sifter, wooden spoon, 20 cm (8 in.) square cake pan lined with aluminum foil, medium mixing bowl, small microwavable bowl, table knife

1 For the bottom layer, place 125 mL (½ c.) butter, the white sugar and egg in the saucepan. Sift the cocoa over the mixture. With an adult's help, stir over medium heat about 1 minute, until slightly thickened. Remove from heat and stir in the graham crumbs, coconut and walnuts. Pat firmly into the pan with your hand. Refrigerate at least 1 hour.

2 For the filling, cream 50 mL (¼ c.) butter in the medium bowl, then add the icing sugar, milk, 8 drops of flavoring and 4 drops of coloring. Mix well. Spread over the bottom layer and refrigerate about 30 minutes, until firm.

3 With an adult's help, melt the chocolate and butter together in the small bowl (page 5). Carefully spread over the filling. Refrigerate about 10 minutes, then cut into squares.

Refrigerate in an airtight container for up to 1 week.

Makes about 2 dozen squares

Hot fudge pudding

A gooey dessert that's even better with ice cream on top.

YOU WILL NEED

250 mL	all-purpose flour	1 c.
75 mL	unsweetened cocoa powder	⅓ c.
5 mL	baking powder	1 tsp.
250 mL	white sugar	1 c.
2	eggs	2
125 mL	milk	½ c.
10 mL	vanilla	2 tsp.
4	squares semisweet chocolate, melted (page 5)	4
90 mL	butter, melted (page 5)	6 tbsp.
325 mL	boiling water	1⅓ c.
125 mL	brown sugar (lightly packed)	½ c.
75 mL	unsweetened cocoa powder	⅓ c.

sifter, medium mixing bowl, large mixing bowl, wooden spoon, 20 cm (8 in.) square cake pan, small mixing bowl

1 Preheat the oven to 180°C (350°F).

2 Sift the flour, 75 mL (⅓ c.) cocoa and baking powder into the medium bowl.

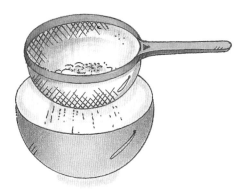

3 In the large bowl, beat together the white sugar, eggs, milk and vanilla. Add the cocoa mixture and the chocolate and butter. Stir until just combined.
Pour into the pan.

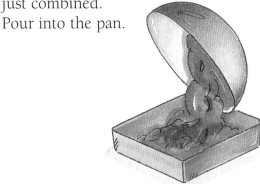

4 In the small bowl, stir together the water, sugar and cocoa. Pour over the batter. Do not stir.

5 Bake 35 to 40 minutes, until a tester inserted into the middle comes out clean. Serve immediately.

Makes 8 servings

Triple chocolate cookies

Three kinds of chocolate packed into every cookie!

YOU WILL NEED

250 mL	margarine (room temperature)	1 c.
175 mL	brown sugar (lightly packed)	¾ c.
125 mL	white sugar	½ c.
2	eggs	2
5 mL	vanilla	1 tsp.
400 mL	all-purpose flour	1⅔ c.
75 mL	unsweetened cocoa powder	⅓ c.
5 mL	baking soda	1 tsp.
2 mL	salt	½ tsp.
250 mL	chocolate chips	1 c.
250 mL	white chocolate chips	1 c.

large mixing bowl, wooden spoon, sifter, small spoon, baking sheet lined with aluminum foil, lifter, cooling rack

1 Preheat the oven to 190°C (375°F).

2 Beat together the margarine and sugars until creamy. Stir in the eggs and vanilla. Sift the flour, cocoa, baking soda and salt over the mixture. Mix well. Stir in the remaining ingredients.

3 Drop the dough by spoonfuls onto the baking sheet about 5 cm (2 in.) apart.

4 Bake 8 to 10 minutes, until firm. Cool 1 minute, then transfer cookies to the cooling rack. Cool completely.

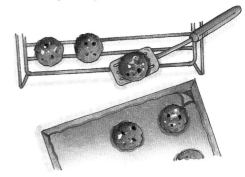

Store in an airtight container at room temperature for up to 1 week or freeze for up to 2 months.

Makes about 4 dozen cookies

OTHER IDEAS

★ Add 250 mL (1 c.) milk chocolate chips, chopped pecans or crushed potato chips.

★ Replace the white chocolate chips with butterscotch or peanut butter chips.

Crunch bars

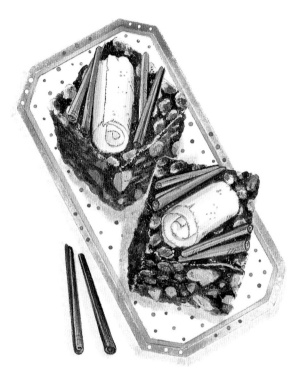

Salty, crunchy, chocolatey good — no baking required.

YOU WILL NEED

375 mL	miniature marshmallows	1½ c.
250 mL	chocolate chips	1 c.
250 mL	peanut butter	1 c.
125 mL	margarine	½ c.
500 mL	crispy rice cereal	2 c.
250 mL	salted peanuts	1 c.

large microwavable bowl, wooden spoon,
20 cm (8 in.) square cake pan lined
with aluminum foil

1 Combine the marshmallows, chocolate chips, peanut butter and margarine. With an adult's help, microwave on high 1 minute, then mix. Microwave another 30 seconds and mix well.

2 Stir in the cereal and peanuts. Pat firmly into the pan with your hand.

3 Refrigerate about 1 hour, until firm.

Refrigerate in an airtight container for up to 1 week.

Makes about 2 dozen squares

DECORATE IT

★ Make chocolate curls for squares or cakes. Hold a wrapped square of chocolate for about 1 minute, until softened. To make wide curls, have an adult help you slowly pull a vegetable peeler along the bottom of the square. To make thin curls, use the peeler on the side.

Chocolate sugar cookies

A chocolate twist on an old favorite.

YOU WILL NEED

250 mL	white sugar	1 c.
125 mL	butter (room temperature)	½ c.
2	eggs	2
25 mL	milk	2 tbsp.
10 mL	vanilla	2 tsp.
550 mL	all-purpose flour	2¼ c.
75 mL	unsweetened cocoa powder	⅓ c.
10 mL	baking powder	2 tsp.
125 mL	colored sugar (optional)	½ c.

large mixing bowl, wooden spoon, sifter, wax paper, rolling pin, cookie cutter, lifter, baking sheet lined with aluminum foil, cooling rack

1 Preheat the oven to 190°C (375°F).

2 Beat together the sugar and butter until creamy. Add the eggs, milk and vanilla. Sift the remaining ingredients over the mixture. Mix well.

3 Following the instructions on page 5, roll out some dough until it is 0.3 cm (⅛ in.) thick. Cut out cookies using the cookie cutter. With the lifter, transfer cookies to the baking sheet, placing them about 4 cm (1½ in.) apart. If you like, sprinkle the cookies with sugar. Repeat with remaining dough.

4 Bake 8 to 10 minutes, until slightly firm. Cool 2 minutes, then transfer cookies to the cooling rack. Cool completely.

Store in an airtight container at room temperature for up to 1 week or freeze for up to 2 months.

Makes about 3 dozen cookies

Blondies

In the mood for a different kind of Brownie? Try this white chocolate version.

YOU WILL NEED

250 mL	white chocolate chips	1 c.
175 mL	white sugar	¾ c.
125 mL	butter	½ c.
2	eggs	2
10 mL	vanilla	2 tsp.
250 mL	all-purpose flour	1 c.
5 mL	baking powder	1 tsp.
250 mL	chocolate chips	1 c.
125 mL	chopped walnuts	½ c.

large microwavable bowl, wooden spoon, 20 cm (8 in.) square cake pan lined with aluminum foil, cooling rack

1 Preheat the oven to 180°C (350°F).

2 Place the white chocolate chips, sugar and butter in the bowl. Microwave about 1½ minutes, until just melted (page 5). Beat in the eggs and vanilla and blend well. Add the flour and baking powder. Mix well, then stir in the remaining ingredients. Pour into the pan.

3 Bake 25 to 30 minutes, until golden brown. Cool completely in the pan on the cooling rack.

Store in an airtight container at room temperature for up to 1 week or freeze for up to 2 months.

Makes about 2 dozen squares

DECORATE IT

★ Stand chocolate cut-outs on cakes, squares or cupcakes. Melt 4 squares of semisweet chocolate (page 5) and spread onto a baking sheet lined with wax paper into a layer about 0.3 cm (⅛ in.) thick. Refrigerate about 15 minutes, until set. Let stand for 5 minutes at room temperature, then cut out diamonds or other shapes with cookie cutters. Stand a cut-out in a dollop of icing on each square.

Midnights

Dark as midnight — and so delicious.

YOU WILL NEED

250 mL	brown sugar (firmly packed)	1 c.
125 mL	butter (room temperature)	½ c.
2	eggs	2
5 mL	vanilla	1 tsp.
375 mL	all-purpose flour	1½ c.
50 mL	unsweetened cocoa powder	¼ c.
2 mL	baking soda	½ tsp.

large mixing bowl, wooden spoon, sifter, small spoon, baking sheet lined with aluminum foil, lifter, cooling rack

1 Beat together the sugar and butter until creamy. Stir in the eggs and vanilla and blend well. Sift the remaining ingredients over the mixture. Mix well. Refrigerate at least 1 hour.

2 Preheat the oven to 180°C (350°F).

3 Drop the dough by spoonfuls onto the baking sheet about 4 cm (1½ in.) apart.

4 Bake 8 to 10 minutes, until slightly firm. Cool 2 minutes, then transfer cookies to the cooling rack. Cool completely.

Store in an airtight container at room temperature for up to 1 week or freeze for up to 2 months.

Makes about 3 dozen cookies

OTHER IDEAS

★ Add 125 mL (½ c.) chopped nuts or chocolate chips, or both.

Crumble muffins

The sweet topping adds an extra kick.

YOU WILL NEED

250 mL	all-purpose flour	1 c.
175 mL	chopped pecans	¾ c.
125 mL	chocolate chips	½ c.
45 mL	white sugar	3 tbsp.
10 mL	baking powder	2 tsp.
5 mL	cinnamon	1 tsp.
1	egg	1
175 mL	chocolate chips, melted (page 5)	¾ c.
75 mL	milk	⅓ c.
45 mL	butter, melted (page 5)	3 tbsp.
50 mL	brown sugar (lightly packed)	¼ c.
50 mL	all-purpose flour	¼ c.
50 mL	chopped pecans	¼ c.
2 mL	cinnamon	½ tsp.
25 mL	butter, melted (page 5)	2 tbsp.

large mixing bowl, wooden spoon, large cereal spoon, muffin pan lined with muffin papers, small mixing bowl, fork, cooling rack

1 Preheat the oven to 190°C (375°F).

2 In the large bowl, combine 250 mL (1 c.) flour, 175 mL (¾ c.) pecans, 125 mL (½ c.) chocolate chips, white sugar, baking powder and 5 mL (1 tsp.) cinnamon. Add the egg, chocolate, milk and 45 mL (3 tbsp.) butter. Stir until just combined. Spoon into the muffin papers so that each is two-thirds full.

3 For the topping, mix the remaining dry ingredients in the small bowl. Add the butter and stir with the fork until the mixture forms coarse crumbs. Sprinkle over the batter.

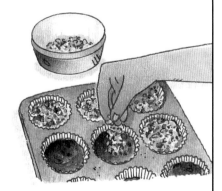

4 Bake 20 to 25 minutes, until golden. Cool 10 minutes in the pan on the cooling rack, then remove muffins from the pan and cool completely on the rack.

Store in an airtight container at room temperature for up to 1 week or freeze for up to 2 months.

Makes 1 dozen muffins

Billionaires

A rich-sounding name for rich-tasting squares.

YOU WILL NEED

250 mL	butter (room temperature)	1 c.
175 mL	brown sugar (lightly packed)	¾ c.
1	egg	1
5 mL	vanilla	1 tsp.
250 mL	all-purpose flour	1 c.
250 mL	quick-cooking (not instant) oatmeal	1 c.
125 mL	chocolate chips	½ c.
25 mL	butter	2 tbsp.
125 mL	chopped almonds	½ c.

large mixing bowl, wooden spoon,
20 cm (8 in.) square cake pan lined with
aluminum foil, cooling rack, small
microwavable bowl, table knife

1 Preheat the oven to 180°C (350°F).

2 In the large bowl, beat together 250 mL (1 c.) butter and the sugar until creamy. Stir in the egg and vanilla. Blend in the flour and oatmeal. Spread evenly in the pan.

3 Bake 30 to 35 minutes, until light golden. Cool 5 minutes in the pan on the cooling rack.

4 While the base is cooling, have an adult help you melt the chocolate chips and butter in the small bowl (page 5). Carefully spread over the base.

Sprinkle the almonds evenly over top. Cool completely on the rack.

Store in an airtight container at room temperature for up to 1 week or freeze for up to 2 months.

Makes about 2 dozen squares

Chocolate shortbread

Use holiday cookie cutters to make special treats for your celebrations.

YOU WILL NEED

250 mL	butter (room temperature)	1 c.
250 mL	icing sugar	1 c.
5 mL	vanilla	1 tsp.
500 mL	all-purpose flour	2 c.
125 mL	unsweetened cocoa powder	½ c.

large mixing bowl, wooden spoon, sifter, wax paper, rolling pin, cookie cutters, lifter, baking sheet lined with aluminum foil, cooling rack

1 Preheat the oven to 150°C (300°F).

2 Beat together the butter and sugar until creamy. Stir in the vanilla. Add the flour and sift the cocoa over the mixture. Blend well.

3 Following the instructions on page 5, roll out some dough until it is 0.5 cm (¼ in.) thick. Cut out cookies using the cookie cutters. With the lifter, transfer cookies to the baking sheet, placing them about 2.5 cm (1 in.) apart. Repeat with the remaining dough.

4 Bake 20 to 25 minutes, until slightly firm. Cool 2 minutes, then transfer cookies to the cooling rack. Cool completely.

Store in an airtight container at room temperature for up to 1 week or freeze for up to 2 months.

Makes about 4 dozen cookies

DECORATE IT

★ Dip cooled cookies halfway into melted dark or milk chocolate (page 5). When the chocolate is set, dip cookies into melted white chocolate so the two chocolates overlap slightly.

Dirt dessert

The tastiest dirt you'll ever eat!

YOU WILL NEED

1	350 g (12 oz.) package chocolate-sandwich cookies	1
1	250 g (8 oz.) package cream cheese (room temperature)	1
250 mL	icing sugar	1 c.
125 mL	butter, melted (page 5)	½ c.
300 mL	milk	1¼ c.
1	113 g (4 oz.) box chocolate instant pudding mix	1
500 mL	whipped dessert topping (prepared as directed on package)	2 c.
24	gummi worms	24

medium-sized, heavy plastic bag; rolling pin; medium mixing bowl; fork; large mixing bowl; spatula; medium clay or plastic flowerpot lined with aluminum foil

1 Place the cookies in the plastic bag and, with an adult's help, use the rolling pin to break them into large crumbs.

2 In the medium bowl, use the fork to blend together the cream cheese, sugar and butter until smooth.

3 In the large bowl, stir together the milk and pudding mix. Using the spatula, gently mix in the whipped topping. Then gently blend in the butter mixture.

4 Place about one-quarter of the pudding mixture in the pot, then one-quarter of the cookie crumbs. Top with 6 gummi worms. Repeat layers until you've used all the ingredients. Refrigerate 1 hour.

Refrigerate covered for up to 1 week.

Makes about 12 servings

OTHER IDEAS

★ If you don't have a flowerpot, serve in a large, clear glass bowl.

★ Omit the gummi worms and stand a clean stem of artificial flowers in the dessert.

Polka-dot pie

A colorful, fun pie that makes any occasion seem like a party.

YOU WILL NEED

325 mL	graham cracker crumbs	1⅓ c.
25 mL	white sugar	2 tbsp.
75 mL	butter, melted (page 5)	⅓ c.
500 mL	milk	2 c.
1	113 g (4 oz.) box chocolate instant pudding mix	1
250 mL	whipped dessert topping (prepared as directed on package)	1 c.
300 mL	multicolored miniature marshmallows	1¼ c.
50 mL	mini chocolate chips	¼ c.
	fork, 23 cm (9 in.) pie plate, large mixing bowl, wooden spoon	

1 With the fork, stir together the graham crumbs and sugar in the pie plate. Add the butter and mix well. Press firmly and evenly against the plate's bottom and sides.

2 Stir the milk and pudding mix together. Gently blend in the dessert topping, 250 mL (1 c.) of the marshmallows and the chocolate chips. Pour into the pie shell and sprinkle the remaining marshmallows on top.

3 Refrigerate 2 hours, until well chilled.

Refrigerate covered for up to 1 week.

Makes about 8 servings

OTHER IDEAS

★ Top each slice with a spoonful of whipped cream. Shake on chocolate sprinkles or colored sugar.

Candy-covered pizza

One great-tasting pizza coming up — hold the anchovies!

YOU WILL NEED

250 mL	chocolate chips, melted (page 5)	1 c.
125 mL	butter, melted (page 5)	½ c.
125 mL	all-purpose flour	½ c.
125 mL	brown sugar (lightly packed)	½ c.
5 mL	baking powder	1 tsp.
2	eggs	2
375 mL	icing sugar	1½ c.
50 mL	butter (room temperature)	¼ c.
25 mL	milk	2 tbsp.
2 mL	vanilla	½ tsp.
	food coloring	
50 mL	sweetened flaked (or shredded) coconut	¼ c.
	candies for decoration	

large mixing bowl, wooden spoon,
large baking sheet lined with aluminum foil,
cooling rack, medium mixing bowl,
table knife

1 Preheat the oven to 190°C (375°F).

2 In the large bowl, mix together the chocolate and butter. Stir in the flour, brown sugar, baking powder and eggs. Blend well. With your hands, pat the dough on the baking sheet into a circle about 30 cm (12 in.) across.

3 Bake 15 minutes, until slightly firm. Cool completely on the sheet on the cooling rack.

4 For the icing, beat together the icing sugar, butter, milk and vanilla in the medium bowl until creamy. Add enough food coloring to tint the icing a color you like. Ice the pizza, then decorate with coconut and candies.

Store the undecorated pizza covered at room temperature for up to 1 week or freeze for up to 2 months.

Makes about 12 slices

OTHER IDEAS

★ Replace the coconut with dried cranberries or other dried fruit.

★ Drizzle the decorated pizza with melted chocolate (page 5) or sprinkle chocolate chips on top.

Icy mousse

A cool, creamy treat that has to freeze overnight, but it's worth the wait.

YOU WILL NEED

1	300 mL (10 oz.) can sweetened condensed milk	1
1 L	whipping cream	4 c.
500 mL	chocolate syrup	2 c.
125 mL	mini chocolate chips	½ c.

medium mixing bowl, electric mixer, wooden spoon, 23 cm x 33 cm (9 in. x 13 in.) cake pan lined with aluminum foil

1 Pour the condensed milk, whipping cream and chocolate syrup into the bowl. Beat with the mixer for about 5 minutes, until the mixture forms soft peaks, as shown. Gently blend in the chocolate chips. Spread evenly in the pan.

2 Freeze about 8 hours, until set.

Freeze covered for up to 1 week.

Makes about 12 servings

DECORATE IT

★ Make chocolate cups for mousse, ice cream or fruit. Using a table knife or small pastry brush, thickly coat the inside of muffin papers with melted chocolate (page 5). Place upside down on a baking sheet lined with wax paper and freeze about 1 hour, until hard. Store covered in the fridge or freezer. Carefully peel off the papers just before using.

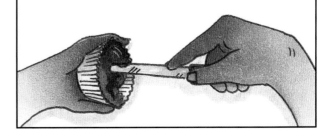

Cupcake cones

Cupcakes in their own edible containers.

YOU WILL NEED

300 mL	brown sugar (lightly packed)	1¼ c.
2	eggs	2
300 mL	milk	1¼ c.
125 mL	vegetable oil	½ c.
5 mL	vanilla	1 tsp.
375 mL	all-purpose flour	1½ c.
150 mL	unsweetened cocoa powder	⅔ c.
5 mL	baking powder	1 tsp.
5 mL	baking soda	1 tsp.
24	flat-bottomed ice cream cones	24

large mixing bowl, fork, sifter, baking sheet, large cereal spoon, cooling rack

1 Preheat the oven to 180°C (350°F).

2 Mix together the sugar, eggs, milk, oil and vanilla. Sift the flour, cocoa, baking powder and baking soda over the mixture and stir until smooth.

3 Stand the cones on the baking sheet and spoon the batter into them, filling each about three-quarters full. With an adult's help, carefully place in the oven.

4 Bake 20 to 25 minutes, until done (page 5). With an adult's help, carefully place the baking sheet on the cooling rack. Cool completely.

Store in an airtight container at room temperature for up to 1 day.

Makes 2 dozen cupcakes

DECORATE IT

★ Fill cupcakes with a surprise before you decorate them. With an adult's help, use a kitchen knife to cut a small cone from a cupcake and cut off its tip. Fill the hole with icing or jam and replace the cone. Ice and decorate.

Chocolate-sandwich cheesecake

Top each slice of this no-bake treat with whipped cream and a cookie.

YOU WILL NEED

1	550 g (19 oz.) package chocolate-sandwich cookies	1
50 mL	butter, melted (page 5)	¼ c.
375 mL	whipping cream	1½ c.
3	250 g (8 oz.) packages cream cheese (softened)	3
250 mL	white sugar	1 c.

medium-sized, heavy plastic bag; rolling pin; medium mixing bowl; fork; 23 cm (9 in.) round springform pan; 2 large mixing bowls; electric mixer; wooden spoon; table knife; plastic wrap

1 Place half the cookies in the plastic bag and, with an adult's help, use the rolling pin to break them into large crumbs.

2 In the medium bowl, use the fork to combine the crumbs and butter. Press evenly over the pan's bottom and place in the freezer.

3 Whip the whipping cream in a large bowl with the mixer until it just forms stiff peaks, as shown.

4 In the other large bowl, beat the cream cheese and sugar until smooth. Break each remaining cookie into 4 pieces and add to this mixture, along with the whipped cream. Gently mix until just blended. Spread over the base.

5 Cover with plastic and refrigerate at least 4 hours, until chilled.

Refrigerate covered for up to 1 week.

Makes about 12 servings

27

1-2-3 cake

As easy as 1-2-3 —
you don't even need a mixing bowl.

YOU WILL NEED

375 mL	all-purpose flour	1½ c.
250 mL	white sugar	1 c.
50 mL	unsweetened cocoa powder	¼ c.
5 mL	baking powder	1 tsp.
5 mL	baking soda	1 tsp.
5 mL	vanilla	1 tsp.
65 mL	butter, melted (page 5)	5 tbsp.
15 mL	white vinegar	1 tbsp.
250 mL	lukewarm water	1 c.

sifter, 20 cm (8 in.) square cake pan
lined with aluminum foil,
wooden spoon, cooling rack

1 Preheat the oven to 180°C (350°F).

2 Sift the flour, sugar, cocoa, baking powder and baking soda into the pan. Make three holes in the mixture. Pour the vanilla into the first hole, the butter into the second and the vinegar into the last one. Quickly pour the water over the mixture and beat well, being careful not to rip the foil.

3 Bake 30 minutes, until done (page 5). Cool 15 minutes in the pan on the cooling rack. Then turn the cake upside down onto the rack and remove from the pan and foil. Cool completely. If you like, make half the Creamy Icing recipe (page 9) and ice the cake.

Store in an airtight container at room temperature for up to 4 days or freeze for up to 1 month.

Makes about 8 servings

OTHER IDEAS

★ Pour only 125 mL (½ c.) lukewarm water over the flour mixture and beat. Stir in 125 mL (½ c.) mashed, ripe banana and bake.

Mud pie

Drop a spoonful of whipped cream and chopped nuts or fruit on each piece.

YOU WILL NEED

325 mL	chocolate wafer crumbs	1¹/₃ c.
50 mL	butter, melted (page 5)	¹/₄ c.
1 L	chocolate ice cream (slightly softened)	4 c.
375 mL	chocolate syrup	1¹/₂ c.
	fork, 23 cm (9 in.) pie plate, large cereal spoon	

1 With the fork, stir together the chocolate crumbs and butter in the pie plate. Mix well. Press firmly and evenly against the plate's bottom and sides.

2 Spoon half the ice cream into the pie shell and spread it smoothly. Pour the syrup evenly over top. Spoon on the remaining ice cream and spread it smoothly over the syrup.

3 Freeze about 2 hours, until firm.

Freeze covered for up to 2 weeks.

Makes about 8 servings

DECORATE IT

★ Serve chocolate-dipped strawberries with pies or cakes. For about 12 strawberries, melt 3 squares semisweet chocolate in a small microwavable bowl (page 5). Use strawberries that still have leaves, and dip each one in the chocolate. Let stand on a plate lined with wax paper until the chocolate is firm. You can also dip orange segments or dried fruit.

Two-bite truffles

Each truffle is two bites of melt-in-your-mouth chocolate richness.

YOU WILL NEED

125 mL	whipping cream	½ c.
250 mL	chocolate chips	1 c.
25 mL	butter (room temperature)	2 tbsp.
25 mL	unsweetened cocoa powder	2 tbsp.

medium microwavable bowl,
wooden spoon, plastic wrap, sifter,
small plate, about 24 paper candy cups

1 With an adult's help, microwave the cream on high for about 2 minutes, until very hot. Stir in the chocolate chips until melted, then blend in the butter until smooth.

2 Cover the bowl with plastic and refrigerate 1 hour, until firm.

3 Sift the cocoa onto the small plate. Form the mixture into 2.5 cm (1 in.) balls and roll them in the cocoa. Coat evenly and shake off any extra cocoa. Place a truffle in each paper cup.

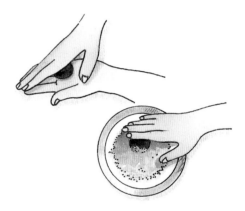

Refrigerate in an airtight container for up to 1 week.

Makes about 2 dozen truffles

DECORATE IT

★ Personalize truffles for a friend. Partially fill a small plastic bag, such as a freezer bag, with slightly cooled melted chocolate (page 5). Cut off a tiny piece of one bottom corner. Twist the bag closed and hold it firmly shut. Squeezing out the chocolate, write your friend's initial on each truffle.

S'more gorp

An easy-to-make trail mix version of S'mores — no campfire required.

YOU WILL NEED

175 mL	mini pretzel twists	¾ c.
175 mL	miniature marshmallows	¾ c.
125 mL	whole natural almonds	½ c.
125 mL	banana chips	½ c.
125 mL	chocolate chips	½ c.
125 mL	raisins	½ c.
	large mixing bowl, wooden spoon	

1 Mix together all the ingredients.

Store in an airtight container at room temperature for up to 3 weeks.

Makes 850 mL (3½ c.) mix

OTHER IDEAS

★ Replace the raisins with your favorite chopped dried fruit.

★ Instead of almonds, use whatever nut you like best.

★ Add 125 mL (½ c.) shredded coconut.

★ Use multicolored or chocolate miniature marshmallows.

Steamin' cocoa mix

Package in an air-tight, mailable container and send to a faraway friend.

YOU WILL NEED

500 mL	instant milk powder	2 c.
175 mL	white sugar	¾ c.
125 mL	coffee whitener powder	½ c.
125 mL	unsweetened cocoa powder	½ c.
2 large mixing bowls, sifter, wooden spoon		

1. In one bowl, sift together all ingredients. Mix well.

2. Repeat step 1, sifting into the other bowl.

Print this note on colorful paper and include it with the mix:

To make a cup of hot chocolate, place 75 mL (⅓ c.) of this mix in a mug, add 250 mL (1 c.) boiling water and stir well. Add marshmallows or a spoonful of whipped cream, if you like.

Store mix in an airtight container at room temperature for up to 2 months.

Makes about 12 cups

OTHER IDEAS

★ For a spicy mix, sift in 5 mL (1 tsp.) ground cinnamon, 2 mL (½ tsp.) ground cloves, 1 mL (¼ tsp.) ground nutmeg and 1 mL (¼ tsp.) ground ginger.

★ Add 6 finely crushed peppermint candies.

★ Make Mocha Cocoa for an adult who likes coffee by adding 75 mL (⅓ c.) instant coffee.

★ Add 250 mL (1 c.) miniature marshmallows.

Silly salami

Ever eaten salami for dessert?

YOU WILL NEED

8	squares semisweet chocolate, melted (page 5)	8
50 mL	butter, melted (page 5)	1/4 c.
45 mL	whipping cream	3 tbsp.
375 mL	shortcake cookie chunks	1 1/2 c.
125 mL	chopped almonds	1/2 c.
75 mL	chopped dried apricots	1/3 c.
75 mL	raisins	1/3 c.
	icing sugar	

large mixing bowl, wooden spoon, wax paper

1 Mix together the chocolate, butter and cream. Stir in the cookie chunks, almonds, apricots and raisins. Refrigerate 30 minutes, until completely cool.

2 Sprinkle a little icing sugar over a large sheet of wax paper. Put the chocolate mixture on the paper and roll into a sausage shape about 25 cm (10 in.) long. Wrap the wax paper tightly around the "salami" and refrigerate 2 hours, until firm.

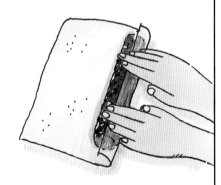

Refrigerate wrapped for up to 5 days or freeze for up to 2 weeks. When you're ready to serve it, let stand at room temperature for about 10 minutes (20 minutes if frozen) before slicing.

Makes about 2 dozen slices

Banana-split loaf

*A split with no ice cream —
but it's just as tasty.*

YOU WILL NEED

250 mL	white sugar	1 c.
125 mL	butter (room temperature)	½ c.
2	eggs	2
5 mL	vanilla	1 tsp.
3	ripe bananas (mashed)	3
50 mL	milk	¼ c.
375 mL	all-purpose flour	1½ c.
50 mL	unsweetened cocoa powder	¼ c.
7 mL	baking powder	1½ tsp.
2 mL	baking soda	½ tsp.

medium bowl, wooden spoon, sifter,
loaf pan lined with aluminum foil,
cooling rack

1 Preheat the oven to 180°C (350°F).

2 Cream together the sugar and butter. Mix in the eggs and vanilla. Add the banana and milk and stir. Sift in the remaining ingredients. Blend well. Pour into the pan.

3 Bake 50 to 60 minutes, until done (page 5). Cool in the pan on the cooling rack for 30 minutes, then remove from the pan and foil. Cool completely on the rack.

Refrigerate covered for up to 1 week or freeze for up to 1 month.

Makes 18 slices

DECORATE IT

★ Make chocolate scribbles for a loaf or cake. Cover a baking sheet with wax paper. Partially fill a small plastic bag, such as a freezer bag, with slightly cooled melted chocolate (page 5). Cut off a tiny piece of one bottom corner. Twist the bag closed and hold it firmly shut. Squeezing out the chocolate, draw scribbles on the wax paper, as shown. Freeze about 30 minutes, until firm, then place on slices of loaf or cake.

Pecan caramel chews

Super-simple, chewy chocolate candies.

YOU WILL NEED

325 mL	pecan halves	1⅓ c.
24	vanilla caramels	24
50 mL	chocolate chips	¼ c.

baking sheet lined with wax paper, small microwavable bowl, wooden spoon, table knife

1 For each candy, place three pecan halves on the baking sheet as shown.

2 Unwrap a caramel and hold it until it's soft enough to flatten into a disk about 3 cm (1¼ in.) across. Carefully press the disk onto the pecans so that they stick together.

3 Repeat steps 1 and 2 until all the caramels are used.

4 With an adult's help, melt the chocolate chips (page 5). Spread a little chocolate on each caramel to mostly cover it.

5 Refrigerate 30 minutes, until firm.

Refrigerate in an airtight container for up to 2 weeks.

Makes 2 dozen treats

OTHER IDEAS

★ Make Bear Paws by replacing the pecans with cashews, as shown.

Haystacks

No-bake goodies that look like
little piles of chocolate hay.

YOU WILL NEED

175 mL	chocolate chips, melted (page 5)	¾ c.
25 mL	butter, melted (page 5)	2 tbsp.
25 mL	milk	2 tbsp.
425 mL	corn flakes	1¾ c.
175 mL	sweetened, flaked (or shredded) coconut	¾ c.

large mixing bowl, wooden spoon, medium mixing bowl, small spoon, baking sheet lined with wax paper

1 In the large bowl, mix together the chocolate, butter and milk.

2 In the medium bowl, break up the corn flakes a little. Mix in the coconut. Add to the chocolate mixture and stir until coated.

3 Place spoonfuls of the mixture on the baking sheet.

4 Refrigerate 2 hours, until firm.

Refrigerate in an airtight container for up to 2 weeks or freeze for up to 1 month.

Makes about 2 dozen cookies

Classic cookie mix

A great gift for a baker.

YOU WILL NEED

425 mL	all-purpose flour	1³/₄ c.
5 mL	baking powder	1 tsp.
5 mL	baking soda	1 tsp.
125 mL	brown sugar (lightly packed)	¹/₂ c.
125 mL	white sugar	¹/₂ c.
50 mL	unsweetened cocoa powder	¹/₄ c.
250 mL	chocolate chips	1 c.
175 mL	chopped pecans	³/₄ c.

sifter, medium mixing bowl, 2 small
mixing bowls, fork, large cereal spoon,
1 L (1 qt.) wide-mouth jar

1 Sift the flour, baking powder and baking soda into the medium bowl.

2 In a small bowl, stir together the sugars.

3 Sift the cocoa into the other small bowl.

4 Packing each layer firmly, spoon half the flour mixture into the jar, then the sugars, then the remaining flour. Spoon the cocoa around the edge of the jar. Add the chocolate chips, then the pecans. Close the lid tightly.

Print this note on colorful paper and tie it to the jar:

1. Preheat oven to 180°C (350°F).

2. Pour cookie mix into large bowl and blend together with your hands. Add 175 mL (³/₄ c.) room-temperature butter, 1 egg and 5 mL (1 tsp.) vanilla. Mix well.

3. With lightly floured hands, shape batter into 2.5 cm (1 in.) balls and arrange about 4 cm (1½ in.) apart on baking sheet lined with aluminum foil.

4. Bake 10 to 12 minutes, until slightly firm. Cool 5 minutes, then transfer cookies to cooling rack. Cool completely.

Store at room temperature for up to 1 month.

Makes about 3 dozen cookies

Minty slice

Top a slice of chocolate or plain pound cake with a scoop of chocolate-peppermint ice cream, then pour on chocolate syrup.

Almond bark

Mix together 750 g (1½ lb.) white chocolate (melted [page 5]) and 500 mL (2 c.) toasted almonds. Pour onto a baking sheet lined with wax paper. Refrigerate 1 hour, until firm, then break into pieces.

Chippy ice cream

Stir mini chocolate chips into softened chocolate ice cream. Spoon into muffin papers and refreeze.

Creamy choco roll

You'll need 500 mL (2 c.) whipping cream (whipped) or 250 g (8 oz.) frozen whipped topping (thawed) and a package of chocolate wafer cookies. Spread a spoonful of whipped cream on a cookie and stand it on its edge. Repeat until you've covered and put together all cookies, as shown. Cover with remaining whipped cream and refrigerate at least 4 hours. Cut slices at an angle.

Angel pudding

Cut angel food cake into cubes, then gently blend into chocolate pudding. You can also use any other kind of cake.

Ice cream cup

Buy or make chocolate cups (page 25) and fill with chocolate ice cream. Top with berries and chunks of your favorite chocolate bar.

Chocolate wrap

Spread peanut butter on a plain flour tortilla, then sprinkle it with chocolate chips. Place a peeled banana near the edge of the wrap and roll it up tightly. Cut in half or in slices.

Ice cream sandwich

Sandwich chocolate ice cream between oatmeal cookies. If you like, roll the sides of the sandwich in chocolate sprinkles.

Chocolate surprise

Brush a thin layer of melted dark or white chocolate (page 5) over a baked pie crust or tart shells. Let it cool before adding the filling, such as pudding or fresh fruit.

Blueberry clusters

Melt 3 squares of semisweet chocolate (page 5). Stir in 375 mL (1½ c.) blueberries. Drop by spoonfuls onto a baking sheet lined with wax paper and refrigerate about 1 hour, until firm. If you like, replace the blueberries with raisins or dried cranberries.

Choco-mint balls

Roll scoops of chocolate ice cream in crushed peppermints.

Chocolate icing

Melt 625 mL (2½ c.) chocolate chips (page 5). Stir in 300 mL (1¼ c.) sour cream and beat until smooth. Cover and refrigerate about 15 minutes, until it is easy to spread. Makes enough to ice a 20 cm (8 in.) round layer cake.

Crunchy pudding

Layer chocolate pudding, chocolate wafer crumbs and banana slices in clear glass bowls or parfait glasses.

Chocolate sauce

Microwave 125 mL (½ c.) milk about 2 minutes, until very hot. Pour into a medium saucepan and mix in 125 mL (½ c.) white sugar and 125 mL (½ c.) unsweetened cocoa powder. Stir over medium-low heat until smooth. Mix in 125 mL (½ c.) chocolate chips until melted. Drizzle over ice cream, cake or fruit. Refrigerate for up to 1 week. Makes 375 mL (1½ c.).